JUST SASSY MAE

JUST SASSY MAE

NATASHA CAMERON

LNC Media Group LLC
Pickerington, OH

JUST SASSY MAE

This book is a work of fiction. Names, characters, places, and incidents are the product of the author's imagination or are used fictitiously. Any resemblance to actual events, locales, or persons, living or dead, is strictly coincidental.

JUST SASSY MAE © 2020 Natasha Cameron

All rights reserved. No part of this publication may be recorded, stored in a retrieval system, or transmitted in any form or by any means, electronic, mechanical, photocopying, recording, or otherwise, without prior written permission from the publisher.

ISBN: 978-1-7363454-0-5

Published by LNC Media Group LLC
Pickerington, OH

Printed in the United States of America
First Edition February 2021

Cover Design by: Make Your Mark Publishing Solutions
Interior Layout by: Make Your Mark Publishing Solutions
Editing: Make Your Mark Publishing Solutions

Contents

Dedication vii

1. Home 1
2. School 12
3. Tattler 25
4. Unfinished Business 32
5. Kitchen Duty 38
6. Announcements 44
7. Decisions 52
8. Pre-game 60
9. The Dance 68
10. Double Trouble 80
11. Back to School 90

About the Author 95

Dedication

This book is dedicated to my husband, who has always supported my dreams. Thanks for all you have done. To my children, for their patience and dedication. To my family and friends, for your endless support. And last but not least, to all the kids in school who struggle to stay right when you want to go left, make wise choices. Thank you, Father, King of Kings. Please continue to pour into me.

Chapter One

HOME

x — x — x — x

'm wrapped like a mummy, and my face is cold. I love it. Waterfalls of drool fall from my mouth and collect on my pillowcase. I'm as snug as a bug in a rug.

"Sassy Mae! Sassy Mae!" Momma yells from the bottom of the stairs. "If I have to come up there to get you, I'm going to drag you down by your legs. Now wake up and get down here. Now!"

"Okay! I'm coming!" I yell back. "Dang," I whisper as I roll over to the other side of the bed, pulling the covers up over my head. I close my eyes and try to go back to sleep, but I know if Momma starts up the stairs, "my days will be numbered," as she likes to say.

I hurry downstairs and into the kitchen.

"Dang, James! You burnt the toast again. Like, how hard is it to make toast?"

I pick up a piece by its corner and hold it close to my face to examine it further. I flip it over to look at the other side. "Yup, just like I thought. Charcoal. I'm not eating this." I fling the toast toward the plate with the rest of the burnt pieces. "Birds wouldn't even choke this down, so how do you expect anyone human to?"

"It's not burnt; it's just a little dark," James

says as he picks up a piece to examine it for himself. He's proud of the toast he made, nodding in approval. Whatever. "If you don't want it, don't eat it." He places the piece of burnt toast back on the plate.

I hop out of my chair to confront him; the chair screeches on the floor and falls behind me. I stand face to face with James, staring him up and down with the meanest look I can muster. "Isn't that what I just said?" I ask, slamming my hand down on the table, making the dishes rattle. "I'm not eating this crap. Now, get it away from me!"

I push the plate of toast down the table with so much force that it slides off the table and hits the floor, shattering.

"Every morning, it's the same stupid crap. James's burnt toast, Millie's thick oatmeal, and Tia's soupy, saltwater eggs. I refuse to keep participating in this deadly breakfast." I back up out of James's face and walk around the table, looking at the slop they call breakfast. "So, the next time you think about waking me up early to eat, Momma, think again."

"Sassy Mae!" Momma shouts.

I cringe. Why can't she just call me Mae?

"Have you gone and lost your mind? You need to learn how to control that attitude of yours before it gets you in trouble. Everyone is not always out to get you."

The room goes silent. You can hear an ant peeing on cotton. It's a little scary.

I walk back, pick up the chair that fell on the floor, and sit back down. James starts to pick up the shattered pieces of plate and burnt toast from the floor. Momma doesn't say another word. She has a creepy smile on her face, which makes me nervous. I know I'm in trouble, but I don't care. Momma wraps her arms around me and ...

SMACK!

I feel a great sting on my backside. "Ahh!" I scream as I jump out of bed.

"Didn't I tell you to get up?" Momma yells. "Now get your tail up and downstairs for breakfast before you are late getting to school."

"Sorry, I'm up!" I rub my backside. "I'm up!"

I get up and get a move on, making my way downstairs before Momma comes back up for round two.

On my way downstairs, I hear dishes clanging in the kitchen, and the smell of burnt toast fills the air. It is just like in my dream. I walk into the kitchen and Momma is placing a pot of water on the stove. I sit down in the squeaky chair and I don't say a word. I dare not repeat the scene that just took place in my dream. I'm sure the outcome would be different this time around. Momma gives me the eye.

I choke on the thick oatmeal and wash it down with the watery eggs. I look over at the toast, which is burnt to a crisp. I can't bear the thought of eating it, so I pass on it. The twins, Millie and Tia, are staring at me. I know they are ready to start trouble. They've been teasing me ever since I can remember, but that's what sisters are for, I guess.

Momma leaves the kitchen. That's their cue to start in on me. It's like clockwork.

The twins are thirteen. Millie is the eldest twin by, like, seven seconds, and she makes sure everyone knows it. She thinks it's her birthright as the older child to boss the rest of us around. Me, on the other hand, I don't take orders so easily, so they like to gang up on me.

"Why are you so quiet, Mae?" Tia (the youngest twin by seven seconds) asks. "You usually don't know how to shut up, but today you haven't said a word." Flashbacks of my dream flood my mind. "Anyways, I hear the dance is coming up at your school, Sassy Mae. Are you going dressed like a bum again?" They all start giggling. "If you want, I can help you with your outfit."

"My name is Mae." I look down at my clothes: a purple, striped shirt with red shorts. "I don't need your help. I can dress myself," I respond.

"You be walking around here looking like nobody loves you, the way you dress yourself. It's just embarrassing." Tia turns the page of her fashion magazine.

"Whatever, Tia! Not only will I go to the dance looking good, but I'm going to win Queen of the Floor too. Plus, what's wrong with what I have on?" I tilt my head sideways and squint at her.

"You just look like … hmm, how can I say this without hurting your feelings? Oh yeah, I can't, so I'm gonna just say it. You're mismatched." She licks her finger to turn the page of her stupid magazine.

Here we go, I think it's my turn. I roll up my sleeves. "I know you're not talking? Sitting over there, looking like you about to audition for the animal channel." Her outfit has a lot of colors and spots. All the pinks and blues hurt my eyes.

"Shut up, Sassy Mae, before I get up and punch you in that smart mouth of yours," Millie (twin number one) threatens. Millie is only mad because she has on the same outfit and looks like she's auditioning too.

I don't reply. I roll my eyes and sit back in the squeaky chair.

✶ ✶ ✶

After breakfast, it is time to go. James and I are walking out the door when Momma reminds us to stay together on the walk.

James is my eight-year-old baby brother who is a freaking nightmare to watch. You would think at eight years old he would have grown out of his baby stage, but he hasn't. He still acts like a baby, and Momma still treats him like one.

✗ ✗ ✗

It's a beautiful, warm day today. The birds are chirping, and the sky is a bright blue. I'm enjoying the peace of the walk when a gust of wind almost knocks me over. A shiny, black-and-blue sports car speeds past us. I look around and James is gone. He's chasing after the car.

"James!" I shout. "Stop running! Momma said we have to stay together."

He continues to run like he is about to

catch up to the car. I take off running after him in fear of getting in trouble. My book bag flops up and down on my back. Sweat runs off my face and down my neck.

"Stop running, James, before I hurt you!" He keeps running like he doesn't hear me. I'm out of breath and my hair is flying in the wind. It's like we are running a marathon to school. James is ahead of me by a couple of feet.

We make it to school, and James runs to his class line by the school's entrance. He looks like he walked the whole way to school. I, on the other hand, am gasping for air, and my hair is a mess.

Chapter Two

SCHOOL

x — x — x — x

The first bell rings, and we are allowed to enter the school, so I book it. I push past the kids in line and run straight to the bathroom. I have to fix my hair. "No running in the halls!" a teacher shouts. But I can't walk. My reputation is on the line and I refuse to give the kids in this school another reason to tease me. So, I run even faster. I can't be caught looking like a hot mess.

Once I make it to the bathroom, I run to the closest mirror to see the damage. It's just like I thought. Strands of my black, curly baby hairs are sticking up all over the place. I start using my fingers as a comb. I run water on my hands and pat my hair to help hold down the hairs that are sticking up.

More kids are entering the school, so I have to move fast. As I continue fiddling with my hair, I hear some girls talking as they stand outside the bathroom doors. They are talking about some new kid to the school. *Not another new kid. Now I really have to fix my hair,* I think as I eavesdrop on their conversation. I look through my book bag for any hair accessories or something that will help tame the frizz. I have nothing, so I get creative.

I wet a paper towel and start to rub it on my hair, hoping this will help flatten the straggly strands. The paper towel crumbles into little pieces. "Aww, now it's worse," I say as I pick the pieces of paper out of my hair. "I give up!" I fling the damp paper towel toward the mirror. "Forget it!" I shout with tears in my eyes.

I have to get to class, and I hope the new kid isn't in my class to see me looking a mess.

When I get to my classroom, I don't see any new faces. *Yes! This gives me enough time to try to get myself together.* I head over to my seat and look at my friend Sparkle's desk. Empty. I scan the room to see if she is sitting somewhere else, and sure enough, there she is bumping her gums to Amber.

Sparkle is my best friend. We have been BFFs since second grade. I was new to the school, and she was the only person who was nice to me or who would even talk to me. I never had to worry about her teasing me about my size or my hair. We became close instantly.

I motion for Sparkle to come over. "Hey! Have you seen or heard about the new kid?" I ask.

"Yeah, girl, the whole school saw him. He's across the hall in Mr. Smith's class with Nyla and Brandi, so you know they are all over him," she replies with her lips poked out.

"Oh, it's a he!" I say as I place my hand over my heart.

"Yeah, girl! I don't know his name, but they say he's okay looking. You know I don't judge."

The bell to start class rings.

"Alright, I'm out, girl." Sparkle gets up and runs to her seat.

⁎ ⁎ ⁎

The day is dragging. Mrs. Finley, our fourth-grade teacher, is saying something about how the human body has enough DNA that it can stretch from the sun to Pluto and back seventeen times. I'm not paying much attention to the lesson.

I almost doze off when the lunch bell rings. It's right on time because my stomach is rumbling. Our class lines up and we head to the lunchroom.

It's pizza day, my favorite day of the week, and I'm ready to chow down. I try to get a glimpse of the new kid but have no luck. Mr. Smith has taken his class outside to eat lunch since it's such a beautiful day.

"Hurry up and eat so we can hit the blacktop; don't you want to see the new boy?" Sparkle asks, stuffing pizza down her throat.

She's right. I'm curious to see what this new kid looks like, so I stuff my pizza in my mouth. We both almost choke on the cheese, but it doesn't stop us.

After we scarf down our food, we hurry to the blacktop. We are on a mission, so we run. We are running so fast that I catch a cramp in my side and have to stop.

"There he goes!" Sparkle says as she tries to catch her breath.

"Where, girl, where?" I yell. I'm bent over and holding my side, panting like a dog.

Sparkle screams, "Be quiet! You're too loud; everyone will hear you. He's over there, on the field playing football." She points with her head, trying not to be noticeable.

"Okay, I'm going over to introduce myself," I say as I stand up straight to walk toward the football field.

I can feel eyes on me as I near the field. I stop and turn around to see who is watching me, and sure enough, Nyla and Brandi are staring me down. I politely wave at them and turn back around to continue walking to the field. I can hear them chattering behind me, but I keep moving. I can see the new kid in the distance; the sun bounces off his light-brown skin. As he runs, the wind blows through his jet-black curls. Everyone's right—he is nice looking.

As soon as I get on the field, I see Johnathon coming my way. I start walking faster so I won't have to talk to him, but he catches up with me.

"Don't bother me, Johnathon," I say, but like always, he doesn't get the message. "Dude! What do you want?"

Johnathon is a four-eyed weasel that's been in my life since I can remember. Our mothers are best friends, so we kind of grew up together. When we were younger, we got along just fine. It wasn't until he started teasing me in front of his loser friends that our issues began. Now we can't stand each other. "What do you want?" I ask again, putting my hands on my hips.

"I just wanted to tell you that you're not his type," Johnathon replies with a smug look on his face.

"Who's type?" I ask, playing dumb.

"The new guy's! You're not fooling anyone. I know you're going over there to ask him out, aren't you?" Johnathon looks down on me over the top of his glasses. "Aren't you?" he asks again.

"No! I'm just going over to introduce myself, loser. Plus, how am I going to like someone I never met?" I look at him like, *duh*.

"Good!" He pushes his glasses up on his face. "Besides, I told him all about you and the rest of the girls in this funky school, and I don't think he would like you."

"What did you say about me?" Curiosity gets the best of me and I want to know.

"I told him the truth about you. That you're a tomboy and a bully with a nasty attitude."

My mouth drops. I can't believe Johnathon would say such awful things about me. I feel like a bull and I can only see red.

"You donkey ass! I'm not a tomboy! I should punch your stupid donkey ass in the face. Talking about me like I'm some kind of bully." My mouth is home to some foul words, but I don't care. Johnathon pissed me off.

His mouth hangs open, and his eyes get big. His glasses fog up. I spin around and stomp away. I head to the swing area where Sparkle is; she was watching the whole thing play out.

"What happened?" Sparkle asks as she jumps off the swing. She's taller than me, so she shades me from the sun. "Why didn't you go to introduce yourself like you said, and why is your face so red?"

I tell her what Johnathon said about me to the new kid.

"What did he say about *me*?" she asks.

I look her up and down. "What's your problem? This isn't about you, Sparkle." I push past her and sit down on the swing.

Sparkle rolls her eyes at me. "Don't catch no attitude with me, honey child. I didn't do nothing to you, so you better get gone with that funky attitude."

I don't mean to snap at her, but I'm still mad about what Jonathon said about me.

"Don't look now, but we've got company."

I know that means Nyla and Brandi are on their way over to be nosey.

Nyla and Brandi are the true definition of mean girls. When we were younger, they used to push me and Sparkle off the swings and throw dirt in our hair on top of teasing us about our clothes.

"What's up? These swings are taken." I jump up off the swing and get in their faces.

"We were just wondering, why were you trying to talk to the new boy? Like, we saw you about to go bother him, so we just wanted to know what you wanted with him," Brandi says through the train tracks in her mouth (Brandi has a mouth full of braces).

Nyla giggles.

"That's none of your business. Y'all are not my momma, and I don't have to answer to y'all. Now back up out of my face, Stank Breath and Brace Face."

I'm not about to back down. I stand up straight.

Nyla rolls her head and looks me up and down. These girls are ready to start some drama, and I'm ready to finish it. "Girl, please. Like, you're not even worth our energy," Brandi states as she grabs Nyla by the arm. They walk away, mumbling and laughing.

The bell rings. Lunch is over, and back to class we go.

The rest of the afternoon, I can't help but think about what happened at lunch and how I let Johnathon get under my skin. The things I said were inappropriate. I should have just kept walking and ignored him.

Chapter Three

TATTLER

I drop my book bag at the door and head to the refrigerator for a snack. Momma stands by the stove, talking on the phone. She is stirring a pot with one hand and holding the phone with the other. The smell of fried chicken fills the house.

"Hey, Momma," I whisper, trying not to interrupt her phone call.

"Hey, Sassy," she replies, turning around

to look at me. "Go get ready for dinner. Where is James?"

I point up with my finger to indicate upstairs.

"Oh, okay. Go wash up and tell James to wash up too."

James is playing a knight tower video game. "Watch my left, watch!" he shouts into his gaming headset.

"Momma said to wash up and get off that stupid game and get ready for dinner before she comes up here to drag you down," I shout into his room.

"He's right behind you, look out!" he continues to yell.

"Did you hear me, James? Momma said get off that stupid game."

"Nooo! I died. I died!" he screams out.

"See what you made me do? You came in here messing with me and distracting me, and I died. Get out! I don't want no stupid dinner!"

"Well, I'ma tell Momma what you said, and you're going to get in trouble. Momma!" I yell from the top of the stairs.

"Okay, okay, you snitch, I'm coming." He puts his controller down.

We still have to wait for the twins to get home before we can eat dinner, so I chill in the family room until then. Momma is still on the phone ("She said *what*, girl?"). I can hear her speaking from the kitchen. Momma talks just as much as Sparkle on the phone.

The twins finally make it home from school.

I hop up, run to the kitchen, and sit in my favorite squeaky chair at the table. The twins wash up and join us. We're all at the table except for Dad. He is always the last one to the table. Momma makes James run upstairs to wake him so we can all eat together.

Dad has been training the night shift at his company, so he sleeps most of the day. He and Momma met in college, but I don't know how because Dad only talks when he's angry.

James takes off, running out of the kitchen. But when I look over at his seat, he's back at the table. "Done," he says without even breaking a sweat. Momma looks at him and shakes her head.

Dad shuffles down the stairs and sits quietly at the table. We say grace and start eating. It's soul food night: fried chicken, baked macaroni and cheese, green beans, and potato salad.

I start slamming. Everything tastes so much better when Momma's helpers aren't involved. I go back for seconds and thirds. I end up being the only one left at the dinner table when I finish. I get up, ready to fly out of the kitchen when Momma stops me.

"Sassy Mae! Come here and sit back down. We need to talk."

Oh no. *What does she want to talk about? Did James tell her I threatened him on the way to school? Or did Johnathon snitch on me?* I sit back down.

"What's this I hear? Is your tail at school cursing like a drunken sailor and calling people out of their name?"

As soon as she asks that, I know it's Johnathon who snitched. That crybaby went home and cried to his momma. Momma is talking, but my mind is stuck on the hurting I'm going to put on Jonathan.

"Do you hear me?" Momma asks.

"Yes," I reply. I missed everything she just said.

"And after you apologize to him, you're going to have kitchen duties for two weeks. If I ever hear those words cross your lips ever again, you're going to wish you didn't have a tongue. You do one more thing, and you can kiss going to that dance goodbye. Do you understand me?" she asks, pointing her finger at my lips.

"Yes," I reply again, hanging my head.

I dash out of the kitchen. I can tell

Momma is furious from the tone of her voice. I don't want her to change her mind and add to my job duty, so I run up the stairs as fast as I can. My eyes fill with tears as I run to my room and shut the door. I hate washing dishes. I ball up my fist and punch my pillow. Johnathon is the cause of this whole mess, and now I have kitchen duty for two weeks.

"Sassy Mae," Momma yells from the bottom of the stairs. "Get down here and clean up this kitchen!"

I bury my head in my pillow and scream. I can't wait to give Johnathon a piece of my mind at school tomorrow.

Chapter Four

UNFINISHED BUSINESS

✗ — ✗ — ✗ — ✗

'm ready. I have mentally prepared myself for the run. I did my hair in two French braids, and I put on my good running shoes. I'm on a mission to get to school fast.

"Don't you want to run to school today, James?" I ask eagerly.

"No, I'd rather walk today," he answers,

as he looks around like he has never seen the sky and trees before.

Great, I think. *The first time I want to run to school, this dude would rather walk. I have to do something. We're walking too slow. Oh, I'll speed walk!*

I start at a medium pace so James can adjust, then I go faster and faster. I'm walking so fast that it's hard for James to keep up without running. My legs are on fire, but I don't care. It just makes me walk even faster. Johnathon and I have some unfinished business.

We are getting closer to the school, so I slow down. I don't want to be out of breath when I get there.

I head to the door where Johnathon enters the school, but he isn't there. Johnathon's mom always drops him off early, so I know he's here somewhere. I search around, trying to find him. The day is not turning out as planned.

Just as I'm about to give up, I spot him over by the breakfast line.

"Johnathon!" I shout as I speed-walk to him. "I have a problem."

"What did I do?" he replies, tilting his head to the side and widening his eyes, acting all innocent.

"You ratted me out, you little weasel. And because you opened your big fat mouth and told your mommy on me, I have kitchen duty for two weeks. Thanks a lot, tattletale!" I shout.

"Well, that's your fault. You shouldn't have been calling me out my name and cursing at me. I believe you should be apologizing to me."

Who does he think he is?

"I see you haven't learned your lesson. So get out my face, or the next time I tell you, you won't be able to leave the house for a week." He fixes his glasses on his nose.

I feel heat rising from the bottom of my feet to the top of my head. I grip the sides of my shorts.

"Did you hear me, tomboy? Get out of my face!"

I cock my hand back and punch Johnathon right in his mouth. It all happens so fast.

"That will teach you for calling me a tomboy," I roar.

Johnathon screams out, "She hit me! She hit me!" He grabs his mouth and tilts his head back. He is acting like he has blood gushing from his mouth.

I can hear Momma's voice in my head: *Sassy Mae, I sent you to school to apologize to that boy, and you turn around and hit him? Kiss that dance goodbye.* I have to think of something quickly. I take a look around to see if any teachers notice Johnathon shrieking. Mrs. Brown, the line monitor, is on her way over to see what the commotion is all about. I have to shut him up.

"Johnathon," I tell him. "Johnathon, you're not even bleeding, so stop screaming." He ignores me. "Okay. If you shut up and don't tell on me, I'll do whatever you say for a week!"

Johnathon instantly stops screaming, dropping his hand from his mouth, "Deal!"

he shouts. He runs off just as Mrs. Brown approaches us. It was all just an act—a scheme in his dirty little plan to take me down. That greasy little weasel struck again.

Chapter Five

KITCHEN DUTY

x — x — x — x

"You apologize to that boy?" Momma asks as she places her hands on her hips.

I back away from her. "No," I whisper.

"What did you say? Did you apologize to that boy?" Momma repeats.

"No! I forgot. Something happened in line when I was going to, and I forgot."

Momma turns and looks at me "Well, go call him now," she instructs.

"Oh, Momma, do I have to? Can I just wait until I see him at school tomorrow?" I plead.

"No!"

I can tell I set her off.

"If you had just done what I asked you to do in the first place, you wouldn't have to call him now, so get moving and do what I asked you to do earlier." Momma points to the phone.

I start moving slowly toward the phone. I don't feel like talking to Johnathon again today. Momma gives me the look of death. I know exactly what that look means: She is ready to dish out punishments. I start moving faster.

I dial Johnathon's home number and ask to speak with him.

"Yes, just a minute," the voice on the other end replies.

"Hello!"

"Hello, Johnathon?" I ask.

"Yes, this is him."

"This is Mae. Sorry for yesterday."

"Well—"

I hang up the phone. I don't care what he has to say. I walk into the kitchen and sit down at the table.

"I'm starving. What's for dinner?" I ask.

"Did you call and apologize to that boy?" Momma asks for the third time.

"Yes, Momma. I called that boy and apologized."

"Don't you sassy me, Mae. Now go wash up for dinner, and hurry back down so you can help me ready the table." Momma waves her hand, shooing me away.

It's taco night and since I'm on kitchen duty, I decide to make it easier on myself and set the table with paper plates and foam cups. I don't want to be in the kitchen all night, washing dishes. Momma sees what I'm doing and gives me that look again.

"Dang," I mumble. I collect the paper plates and foam cups from the table and re-set the table with the real dishes.

James is about to make his usual sprint upstairs to wake Dad up when I volunteer to.

"Okay, Sassy Mae, go wake your dad," Momma says.

I knock on the bedroom door, but there is no answer. I knock again. I hear a sleepy noise from the other side of the door.

"It's dinner time," I say through the door.

There is no answer. I go back downstairs.

It takes Dad longer than usual to come down for some reason. He must have been exhausted. When he finally comes downstairs, we are all withering away from starvation.

After dinner, I ask Momma if she needs help with anything once I'm finished cleaning the kitchen.

"Sure I do, but first we eat dessert," she answers.

Momma gets up from the table and places a double-layered, extra-chocolate fudge cake on the table. My mouth waters.

"Mae, grab the plates out the cabinets," Momma instructs as she cuts a slice of cake. I run over to the cabinets and grab the paper plates. I know Momma's about to get on me, but she doesn't seem to notice or care. Everyone is focused on the cake. No extra dishes for me to wash!

I clean the kitchen and help Momma with organizing the pantry. It feels good to help, so I go room to room and ask everyone in the house if they need help with anything. The twins need help cleaning their room, James needs help finding batteries for his gaming remote, and Dad asks for me to read a book. It's a tough job, but I manage to help everyone, and it's a good feeling; the satisfaction I feel is well worth it.

Chapter Six

ANNOUNCEMENTS

"Students, please be on your best behavior so your dance privileges won't get revoked."

Mrs. Finley announces to the whole class that there is going to be a talent show with the dance on Friday. Cheers break out in the classroom. A talent show with a dance! I look at Sparkle, and she is staring back at me. We both nod at the same time; we're thinking the same thing. We are going to tear up that dance floor.

I think about what I'm going to wear and what dance Sparkle and I are going to do for the talent portion of the dance. Mrs. Finley begins the lesson; this time, it's math, fractions, and decimals. I feel like I'm not missing anything important, so I do what I do best: I wander off to la-la land.

I'm in the lunchroom, scarfing down my food so I can run to the playground when the new boy approaches my table, shaking his curly locs.

"Hello, Mae," he says, smiling with a twinkle in his eye.

I smile back. "Hello." We lock eyes.

"Will you go to the dance with me?" he asks as he pulls up a chair.

"Yes!" Food hangs out of my mouth. "Yes!"

Nyla and Brandi are a table over, watching the whole thing play out. One of them begins to cry, which makes me smile wider. Next thing I know, the new kid leans in toward me like in the movies. I lean in toward him.

"What do you think, Mae? Mae, what do you think?" I drift back to reality. Mrs. Finley is asking me a question. "What do you think?" she asks again.

I have no idea what she's talking about because I wasn't paying attention. I look over at Sparkle, and she shakes her head.

"No," I answer.

"Good job, Mae, you're right. You can't add fractions with different denominators."

I better stay focused, I think, but a minute later I drift back to la-la land. I'm at the dance. The lights are flashing, and the music is popping. I'm rocking my hips and snapping my fingers. I'm dancing better than I ever have before and I'm crowned Queen of the Floor. Everyone cheers my name.

"Mae, Mae, Mae!"

"Mae? Mae, excuse me, Mae!" Mrs. Finley is seeking my attention. "Save it for the dance on Friday."

I was popping and dancing in my seat. The entire class bursts out laughing. I sink down in my chair.

✖ ✖ ✖

At lunchtime, Sparkle and I are in the corner of the playground going over our moves. Sparkle has the meanest spine pop drop move I've ever seen. She said she had to watch the same New Viewers Tubers video over and over again until she mastered it.

Out of the corner of my eye, I see Johnathon. He's walking our way.

"What do you want? Don't come over here messing with us. Don't you have something better to do?" I ask, but he keeps on walking.

I remember then that I still owe him a week's worth of favors, and he's probably coming to collect.

"What do you want?" I ask again.

I whisper something under my breath about Johnathon's glasses. Sparkle laughs. *Dang, she must have heard me.*

"What do I want? We have an agreement, or did you forget that fast?" he asks with a smug look on his face. "Anyways, I want to use one of my favors. That's why I came over."

I sigh. "What is it?"

"I want you to go to the dance with me. I figured since you have such a nasty attitude, and nobody is going to ask you anyway, you could go with me."

Oh, hell no! What is he thinking? We don't even like each other, but I have to think about the talent show dance. I don't want him to tell on me.

"Okay, Johnathon, I'll go to the dance with you." I grip the sides of my shorts. Johnathon's jaw drops. He looks like a deer in headlights.

Finally, he closes his mouth and nods. "I have another favor I want to use."

The nerve of him, trying to use two favors in one day. I clench my teeth together. "Okay, what?" I reply.

"I want us to go dressed alike in the same colors."

I roll my eyes.

Sparkle bursts out laughing and hits the ground rolling. She holds her stomach and tears run down her face. I shoot her a dirty look, but that doesn't seem to stop her from laughing. She gets on my nerves sometimes.

Johnathon walks away, smiling.

"Girl! Why do you look like somebody done farted in your face?" Sparkle sputters out as she continues to laugh.

"Shut up, Sparkle! Before I tell him you like him and that you put hearts around all his pictures in the yearbook."

The laughter stops, and her smile drops. "Go ahead. I dare you! Because if you do, I'll tell the new boy you like him," she counters.

I roll my eyes and suck my teeth. We continue to practice our moves.

Chapter Seven

DECISIONS

x — x — x — x

"Sassy Mae, come in here!" I roll my eyes. *What now?* I think. I enter the kitchen and sit at the table. Momma is hanging up the phone.

"I was just on the phone with Deborah, and she said you and Johnathon decided to go to the dance together and dress alike. Is this right?" she asks. "This doesn't sound like you. Did you do something to that boy that you are not telling me about, Sassy Mae? You did apologize, didn't you?" She narrows her eyes at me. "You're up to something, and I'm gonna find out."

I don't reply.

"Don't just sit there and act like you don't hear me talking to you, Sassy Mae." She gives me the eye.

I grab my head with both hands and push it down on the table. "Nothing's going on."

"Now, you know your dad isn't about to go for this going-to-the-dance nonsense. I'm glad y'all made up, but don't think you're about to go to some dance with a boy. I don't care who it is!"

"I know, Momma," I say, pushing my head even farther down on the table.

"I know you know, and that's why I told

Deborah y'all done lost y'all's dang minds and that you are flying solo. It's not even that type of party."

My eyes grow in disbelief. I'm not sure what is going to happen now that Momma told Johnathon's mom we are not going to the dance together. Johnathon better not try and play me and tell my momma on me because if I get in trouble and can't go to the dance, I'll put a world of hurt on that boy.

The dance is tomorrow, and I have no idea what Johnathon wants us to wear. Is he going to call the whole thing off and just tell my momma I hit him since Momma canceled plans with his mom? I still plan on going to the dance dressed like Johnathon, despite what Momma said. Just then, the phone rings and I run to answer it.

"Hello?"

"May I speak to Mae, please?" the voice on the other end asks.

"This is me, what's up?"

The sweet voice on the other end of the phone changes. It's Johnathon. "You ready to hear what we are wearing tomorrow?"

The plan is still in motion. I release some air; he's not calling to tell on me. There is a long pause.

"What?" I ask, looking up at the ceiling with my head tilted. There is still no response. "What?" My patience is running thin; I don't have time for these games. "Spit it out already!"

"Okay, okay, are you ready?"

Johnathon knows how to push my buttons. I take a deep breath. "I'm ready." I slowly remove the phone from my ear.

"All blue, with white shoe—"

I hang up. I got what I needed and don't need to hear Johnathon's voice a second longer.

"He's so immature," I say as I run upstairs.

All I need to do now is figure out what I am going to wear. I hear the phone ringing again. "That better not be Johnathon," I say under my breath. I'm sitting on the edge of my bed, trying to think of something in my closet that's blue. I have a rainbow of colors but nothing solid blue. "Telephone, Mae," James yells from downstairs.

"I'm busy!" I shout back. I already know who's on the other end of the line.

I've been searching for hours when Momma walks into the room. "This should work for you," she says with a smile. She holds out a tired, old, red dress shirt with ruffles on the sleeves. "It's your favorite color!"

The shirt looks like it has been in her closet since she was ten years old. I turn up my face. I can smell the mothball odor coming off the shirt. I look at Momma's face and see she's looking at me, so I force myself to smile.

"Thanks, Momma," I reply.

"Girl, don't be giving me the stank face! This shirt is nice. I wore this shirt to my first school dance, and it made all the girls jealous."

Just like I thought—it's been in her closet for years.

"This shirt is perfect for you." She lays the red shirt across my bed.

"Thanks again, Momma. I'll find something to wear with it," I say as she leaves the room.

I sit back on the edge of my bed. What was I thinking, telling Momma I would wear this smelly old shirt? I have no intention of wearing this red shirt. It's not even the color Johnathon wants us to wear.

I hear a snort from the doorway. Tia stands there with her hands on her hips.

"You better clean that mess up before Momma or Daddy sees it."

I look around and notice everything from my closet and drawers are on the floor.

"I told you if you needed my help, I would help you," Tia says. She crosses her arms and smirks.

I smile as I stand up. "Will you help me? Please."

Tia's eyes light up, and I can see all the teeth in her mouth. "Okay. Let me go talk to Millie, and I'll be back." She bolts out of my room. When she comes back, she is holding the perfect outfit.

Chapter Eight

PRE-GAME

X — X — X — X

I don't want to hurt Momma's feelings, so I stuff Tia and Millie's shirt in my book bag. I put the mothball shirt on to leave the house. I have it all planned out. When I get to school, I will change out of the red shirt and into the blue shirt. It's a genius plan.

I make it to school in one piece. Once I arrive, I spot Johnathon. He's wearing an all-blue shirt with blue jeans. He is looking around like he is searching for someone. I can't take any chances of him seeing me in my red shirt before I change. Knowing Johnathon, he will call his mom to tell on me. I have to avoid him just in case he's looking for me. I duck down and creep around to the back of the school. I'm moving like a ninja; no one sees me. Once I make it to the rear of the school, I try to lie low.

"Hi," I hear behind me. I turn around to see who's speaking. It's the new kid.

"H-hi," I stutter. I look down at my feet to avoid eye contact.

"I'm Lavelle. I'm in Mr. Smith's class," he says, smiling.

"Yeah, I know who you are. The whole school does. I mean, when we get a new student, they announce it to the whole school over the announcements," I reply, looking up at his face.

He smiles again and I smile back.

"What's your name?" he asks.

"Mae," I reply.

"Right! Johnathon gave me the rundown on all the kids in our grade." He chuckles.

"Then why did you ask my name if you already knew?" I ask, confused.

"You can't believe everything you hear, so I was making sure I had it right."

I smile even wider. *Not only is he cute, but he's smart*, I think.

"You've got on red today! I thought you and Johnathon were supposed to match, but he has on blue today … Did something change?" he asks.

My smile vanishes; I open my mouth to respond, but he interrupts me.

"I saw you punch Johnathon on the playground the other day. You have a mean right hand. Are you one of them mean girls? I thought you'd be—"

"What's up with all the questions? Are you the police or a snitch? Are you going to tell on me?"

He laughs. "Are you going to punch me?" He raises his hands and backs up.

I give him my mean eyes. "No! I'm not gonna punch you," I answer.

"I'm just playing." He smiles. "I don't think you're a mean girl." He drops his hands as he walks back toward me.

My smile comes back, and I ease up on the eyes.

"Hey, what are y'all talking about?" I hear from a distance.

I know exactly who that is: Quad Eyes. Johnathon is walking toward us, looking all goofy. "So much for lying low," I whisper.

"Hey, what are y'all talking about?" he repeats as he gets closer.

I turn around and act like I don't hear or see him. I need to escape.

Lavelle responds, "Nothing much, just talking to …"

When they turn around, I'm gone. I duck off and hide behind a trash bin next to the school. I watch as they look around for me. I have to make another escape—and fast.

My eyes start to burn from the horrible smell coming from the trash bins. It smells like rotten eggs and dookie. I close my eyes to shield them from the funk. I look back up and realize Johnathon and Lavelle are gone. The coast is clear. I pop up from behind the bins and dash around the corner of the school.

"Now, don't you look nice."

It's Brandi and Nyla. I'm not ready for any more drama this morning.

"Yeah, you do look nice, and you smell nice too," Nyla says sarcastically.

Nyla and Brandi slap hands.

"So, like, I see you let your mother dress you today, and she let you wear some of her smelly perfume."

I roll my eyes as they laugh. I have to stay focused on the dance. I loosen my clenched fists. Luck is on their side today. I walk up to them and put my finger in both of their faces.

"Look, you don't want this problem with me right now, so y'all better back off. Period." I take my finger out of their faces, cross my arms, and lean back.

"Oh no, you didn't put your crusty finger in my face, little girl," Brandi says with raised eyebrows.

Nyla rolls her neck with her finger up. "Yeah, like, who do you think you are?"

I can't keep arguing over the same stuff. I have things to do before I run into Quad Eyes again.

"Whatever," I say as I push past them.

"Yeah, you better run," one of them shouts as I walk away.

I manage to find time to change out of the red shirt and into the blue one. I look around the classroom and realize Sparkle isn't here yet. *Where could she be?* I thought she knew today was the talent show dance. I sigh.

As class goes on, there is still no Sparkle. It's lunchtime, and still no Sparkle. My friend is missing. Now who will I perform with at the dance? I have to accept that she isn't going to make it. My brain starts to hurt. I'm thinking about things way too hard. I have to calm down and stop worrying. I come up with the conclusion that I'll rework the moves and dance by myself.

At lunch, I practice by the trash cans, trying to get it right. Everyone is staring at me, but I keep working. I'm stuck on the spin move Sparkle was showing me, and I have no idea what to do. My dream of winning Queen of the Floor is slipping out of my grasp.

Chapter Nine

THE DANCE

x — x — x — x

I can hear music playing from the gym. I'm super geeked. The gym lights are off, but I can see colors of flashing lights hitting the floor. I run to the dance floor. "No running," a teacher shouts, but again it's too late. I'm already in the middle of the dance floor. I start moving and popping, shaking and dropping. I can't stop dancing.

It's almost time for me to take the stage

in the talent show. I go backstage to practice the part that has me defeated when Brandi and Lavelle walk up.

"What do you want?" I ask.

"We came over here to help you. We saw you at lunch, working on your moves. And well … like, I just wanted to try and help," Brandi replies.

"Why?" I ask, frowning. "Why do you want to help me? You don't even like me."

"For the record, it's you that doesn't like me," she says. I raise my eyebrow. "Like, every time Nyla and I try to approach you, you're either screaming dirty names at us or jumping in our faces."

I almost snap at her, but I pause to think. She's right. I do react like that. All this time,

I thought they were the mean girls. Could it really be that I'm the mean one?

"What about the time you pushed me off the swing and threw dirt in my hair?" I ask.

"We were young, and I'm sorry about that," she says.

"I'm sorry too," I say, and we smile at each other.

"Now let us show you this move." Brandi gets up, spins around, and shows me what I've been doing wrong. Lavelle shows me the pop move. Everything is turning out perfect, and Brandi is way cooler than I thought.

"See what happens when you let your guard down?" Lavelle says as he nudges me.

As I near the stage, my heart starts beating fast. I can hear it over the audience. I look over at Brandi. Can I really pull this off without Sparkle? I walk on to the stage and I'm instantly glued to the spot. My legs are noodles. The music starts.

"Move it!" Brandi yells.

I snap out of it, close my eyes, and start dancing. I feel free and I put every piece of energy and emotion inside me on the stage. I execute the move Brandi and Lavelle showed me flawlessly. I'm breathing heavy, and I open my eyes. I did it! I did it. The whole crowd cheers.

I jump up and down and run off the stage. It's just like how I pictured it to be. I'm sure to win Queen of the Floor now.

✶ ✶ ✶

I've worked up a thirst, so I head over to the concession stand to grab a free bottle of water.

"I like your outfit! Are you ready for our dance?" It's Johnathon. "Have you been trying to avoid me?" he asks, looking down at me from over his glasses with that goofy face I hate.

My nose wrinkles. "Yup. That's what I've been doing."

The music starts back up. "You know the deal. It's time for you to dance with me!" he shouts over the music.

"You didn't say anything about dancing with you," I shout back.

"Well, I'm saying it now! As a favor, I want you to dance with me." I'm so fed up with Johnathon and his shenanigans. "No!" I scream.

Johnathon looks at me. His eyes grow wide and his eyebrows lift. I guess he didn't think I would say no, but I'm sick of him. He is clearly abusing his power. His eyebrows turn in.

"If you don't dance with me, I'm going to tell your mom you put your hands on me."

It feels like thorns are stabbing my skin. I decide to hold up my end of the bargain and be nice. "Fine, you little weasel," I whisper.

"What? I didn't hear you," he shouts.

I nod at him. His face lights up like a Christmas tree, and his smile stretches from ear to ear. I'm upset with myself. Why didn't I just listen to Momma and apologize? I had to let my anger get the best of me.

I continue to the concession stand for that bottle of water. Once I quench my thirst, I hit the dance floor with Johnathon. I'm ready to get this over with. I turn and look at Johnathon as we dance; he starts flopping around like a fish. I don't know who taught him how to dance, or if he's dancing or dying. It's kind of funny, and I almost crack a smile.

The DJ stops the music in the middle of the song to make an announcement. "Please, students, no inappropriate booty-shaking of any kind and remember to be at least three feet apart." The DJ starts the music back up but plays a different song.

"Well, nice dancing with ya," I shout over the music. I give Johnathon the deuces sign and walk away, smiling. His face turns from pink to red like I'm the Mae who stole Christmas.

"Get back here! You ripped me off, tomboy, and I'm telling your momma on you!"

I stop dead in my tracks, turn around, and scowl at him. I walk up to him and get in his face.

"I tried to be nice to you," he said. "But you just don't learn. So, now you get what you deserve. By the way, I have one more thing for you."

Johnathon points his sausage-looking finger in my face. I clench my fists.

"What?" I ask, squeezing the word through my teeth. I step in closer so I won't miss a word he says.

SMACK!

Stinging pain shoots across my face like lightning, and my eyes water. Johnathon just slapped me. "Aww!" I scream out.

I'm in attack mode. I swing my arms around and grab him by his shirt. I ball up my fist and let loose on his face. I start spinning him around while dodging his hits. We end up in the middle of the dance floor. He's got me pinned down, and I can't get up. I lift my legs and wrap them around his body, pulling him down. I get up and place him in a headlock. I start punching him with the other hand. He is strong and isn't going down quickly. He gets out of my headlock and places me in a wrestling hold. He has me pinned down, and I can't move. I start to fight dirty. I grab his hair, but it's too straight. It slips through my hands. I grab for it again and this time I wrap it around my fingers and pull. He screams.

"Get off me! Get off me!"

I hold on tight. Johnathon lets me out of his wrestling hold and grabs my hair and pulls. I want to scream so badly, but I stay strong. We are sliding and rolling all over the floor.

"Fight! Fight! Fight!" someone yells out as we tumble around the gym floor. I finally get him down again, and I place one of his hands underneath my knees as I climb on top of him. I pull my hand back and ball up my fist, swinging it toward his face with all my might. It's going to be lights out for him. Just as my fist is about to hit his face, a teacher catches it. The teacher pulls me off of him.

"To the principal's office, now!" The teacher yells as she pushes me toward the gym's exit doors.

I flop down in one of the ugly orange chairs in the principal's office. The principal stares at me with her arms crossed. My file is open in front of her, but she isn't concentrating on it. I can't tell what she is thinking. I melt in the chair.

"I should suspend you right now. But I talked to your parents, and we came up with an alternate solution. Your behavior is shameful and unacceptable. You need to learn how to conduct yourself better. Just shameful." She shakes her head. "Your punishment is as follows. You will have in-school suspension for a week with the loss of all your school privileges for the rest of the year." She takes a breath. "And the next time you get sent to my office for any reason other than positive achievements, you will be suspended for five days flat. Do you understand me?"

"Yes," I say, hanging my head.

"You're excused. Go sit in the office until your mother comes to get you." She closes my file.

Momma picks me up, and I can tell from her raised eyebrows that she is mad. The only thing she says to me on the ride home is, "Nice shirt." I still have on the blue shirt the twins picked out for me. I didn't have time to change out of it like planned. I sigh, knowing Momma is disappointed.

Chapter Ten

DOUBLE TROUBLE

x — x — x — x

take off the shirt and hang it up in the twins' closet. I wash up for dinner and head to my room. I don't have an appetite today. Dinner is a quiet one for me. It's spaghetti night. Once everyone finishes eating, I clean the kitchen up and turn to go upstairs.

"Come and sit down," Dad says as he pats the seat cushion next to him.

He is sitting in the family room. I sit down beside him, and we just sit there quietly until the doorbell rings. Dad tells me to go answer the door. When I open it, my jaw drops. It's Johnathon and his momma. I want to shut the door on them and run and hide. Dad comes up behind me.

"Come on in," he says, moving me out of the way.

Why are they here, and what do they want? I know I'm in trouble, but I didn't think we were going to have a group sit-down. We all enter the family room and I look at Johnathon, who's looking down at the floor. He looks like a sad puppy dog. I peer over at our moms and see disappointment on their faces, so I decide to join Johnathon and his pity party and hang my head as well.

"Now that we are all together, we can get to the bottom of things because I need to know what the problem is here. One minute everything is all cool, and the next y'all are fighting like cats and dogs. Am I missing something here? And before someone thinks they are going to answer "Nothing" or "I don't know," I am going to ask this one more time: What seems to be the problem?" Dad asks.

Johnathon and I both start talking at the same time.

"One at a time," Dad says, stopping us from speaking. "Johnathon, you first."

I'm upset. Why does Johnathon get to go

first? What happened to ladies first? All he is going to do is blame me for everything.

"Well, the other day at school, we were playing when Mae cussed at me, then she slapped me and started calling me names," Johnathon explains, looking at me the whole time.

He is right. I did do all those things and probably more, but he's not so innocent either.

"Okay, your turn, Mae," Dad says, pointing to me.

"Okay, first of all, he always calls me a tomboy and when I tell him to leave me alone, he doesn't listen. And he slapped me in my face at the dance for no reason!" I say, staring back at Johnathon.

"This has got to stop!" Dad says, his voice

scarily calm. "Y'all have been friends your whole lives. Heck, your mommas are friends, so y'all might as well be family, and family doesn't fight. Family or not, y'all shouldn't be fighting at all. If I were in my right mind, I would ground both of you for life." Dad looks at both of us. "At school, acting like hooligans. I don't know what to do with y'all; I just don't know." Dad starts pacing back and forth.

He places his finger against his lip and looks over at Momma, who's sitting next to Johnathon's mom. He continues to walk and think. "I'm conflicted. Maybe y'all can help. What do you think your punishment should be?" Dad asks, looking at us.

I'm confused. I was expecting an hour-long rant about right and wrong. Maybe extra chores or something. But to come up with my own punishment and torture myself? That is new to me. I am not down with this form of brutality.

"Johnathon," Dad says. "What do you think your punishment should be?"

Johnathon is looking all weird, and then he answers, "Umm … No TV, video games, or electronics for a week."

Dad nods. "That sounds great, very good. But let's make it two weeks if your mom agrees?" Dad looks at Deborah.

"That's fine with me," Deborah replies.

That spoiled brat! He gets off with a slap on his hand. It's my turn, and all eyes are on me.

"Umm … Umm …" I can't do it; I can't come up with my punishment.

Dad gives me the evil eyes, so I think of something quick.

"Umm ... no outside privileges for a week," I say, playing it safe.

"That's a start. How about no electronics, TV, or dessert for two weeks? Oh, and you're going to do a book report on Claudette Colvin since you want to fight for no reason. At least have a good reason to fight. And I want it by next week," Dad adds.

"What?" I yell out. I backtrack when I see the look on Dad's face. "I mean, yes. Okay."

Momma walks Johnathon and his mom to the door. I sit there with my heart bleeding in my hands. I'm angry, sad, and frustrated all at the same time. I get up from the couch. Dad stops me and makes me sit back down.

"Your mom told me you called that boy out his name. You should have gotten grounded for that, but you got off easy by just having to apologize to him. And from the look of things, it seems you couldn't even do that right. I'm disappointed in you, Mae. If you would have kept your head in those books and not on any and everything else, you wouldn't even be in this mess. You deserve that punishment for being so dang hardheaded. So, hear this: The next time you decide to disobey your mother or me, it will be your last time. Do you hear me?" Dad asks in this deep voice.

"Yes," I answer with tears in my eyes.

"Now, get your butt up to your room, and don't come out for the rest of the week." Dad shakes his head in disappointment.

I hop off the couch, run to my room, and flop on my bed. I bury my head in my pillow and start crying. Dad is right. Everything is all my fault. I called Johnathon out his name, I punched him, and I disobeyed Momma. I cry even harder.

Momma walks into my room. "Stop crying," she says as she wipes my tears away. "There is a lesson to be learned here, you know. You can't be angry or sassy all the time. You need to learn how to control your anger. Now, I'm not saying let people take advantage of you or hit on you, but you need to learn some things aren't worth the fight. Just look at the mess you made. Some things you just have to ignore. Now, go to sleep. You will feel much better in the morning. Oh, and one more thing. You have an extra week of kitchen duty for that shirt stunt you pulled."

Momma's right. With all my punishments from home and school, and not winning Queen of the Floor, I have definitely learned my lesson. I wipe my eyes and go to sleep.

Chapter Eleven
BACK TO SCHOOL

x — x — x — x

It's Monday morning, and my life sentence starts today. I drag myself out of bed and downstairs to eat breakfast. Laughter and cheer fill the air, but all I feel is gloom and despair. I sit at the table and choke down what feels like my last meal.

On the walk to school, my legs become heavier and heavier. I'm still sad and angry with myself over last week. I make it to school, and I head over to the all-black double doors. These are the doors where I'm to enter my sentence every day for a week. These doors are also known as the "bad kid entrance."

I stop and bend down to tie my shoe. They are already tied, so I untie them just to re-tie them. I'm stalling for time. I look up and notice Sparkle walking toward me. I have a bone to pick with her.

"Sparkle, what happened to you Friday?" I ask.

"Girl! I called you, and your brother said you were busy. What happened at the talent show dance? Did you win? And why is

Johnathon telling everyone he kicked your butt? He said he kicked your butt so bad that you went home crying to your momma," she says as she continues to walk toward me. "Girl, let me see your lip; he said he busted it up good!"

She is examining my face.

I can't believe Johnathon. After all that we just went through and all the trouble we are in, why he would spread rumors like that? "Oh no, he didn't! Where is he at?" I ask.

I am ready for round two. Sparkle points to him, and we walk toward him.

"Johnathon!" I shout.

As he turns to face me, I remember the things Brandi said to me at the dance and how Johnathon hates being called names.

Johnathon raises his eyebrows at me.

"Sorry for all the name calling and if I ever hurt your feelings," I tell him.

Everyone around us gasps. I turn and walk away feeling great, even though I know this won't be the last of Johnathon and his shenanigans.

THE END

About the Author

Born in Akron, Ohio, Natasha Cameron's imagination grew as a child. Moving from town to town, she experienced many different childhood  issues. As a solution to her problems, she began to entertain her peers with jokes and stories. Over the last few years, she became a devoted wife and a mother to five beautiful children. As a mother, she uses those same jokes and stories to entertain her children. Now, she has welcomed the world with her *Just Sassy Mae* series.

KEEP IN TOUCH WITH NATASHA CAMERON

Website: www.justsassymae.com

Facebook: NJ Author Cameron

Thank you for reading *Just Sassy Mae*

If you enjoyed this book, please help spread the word and leave an online review.

Made in the USA
Monee, IL
05 August 2021

74356879R00069